Dragonis

DRAGONISH

By Emma Simon

With an introduction by
Caroline Bird

THE EMMA PRESS

To Mum, who kept her books for me

ॐ

Sometime we see a cloud that's dragonish,
A vapour sometime like a bear or lion,
A towered citadel, a pendent rock,
A forkèd mountain, or blue promontory
With trees upon't that nod unto the world
And mock our eyes with air.

Antony and Cleopatra, Act 4, Scene 14

———————

THE EMMA PRESS

First published in Great Britain in 2017 by the Emma Press Ltd

Poems copyright © Emma Simon 2017
Introduction copyright © Caroline Bird 2017

ISBN 978-1-910139-64-6

A CIP catalogue record of this book
is available from the British Library.

Printed and bound in Great Britain
by Airdrie Print Services, Glasgow.

The Emma Press
theemmapress.com
queries@theemmapress.com
Birmingham, UK

Introduction

It's morning and as you drift up from sleep you linger for a moment, half-submerged inside a dream. This is the liminal space that Emma Simon's poems occupy. Objects are animate. Time is tangible. Days can be plaited like braids, dismantled like tractors or flown like kites. If you tune your ears correctly, voices rise from unusual places: cockroaches, trees, tennis rackets, even the electronic scales speak a language of loss. These are not fanciful illusions, but dangerously real. Just as dreams reflect and comment upon our everyday lives, these poems weave their worlds from ordinary images, re-appropriated. Halos are looped through the wallpaper. Smiles run in the rain. *Dragonish* reminds us to squint our eyes and look again, to see life as it surreally is. You're at home, you recognise these walls and yet something is different, untethered… there was a dragon in your dream… and now there is ash in the air…

Caroline Bird

February 2017

Contents

The Parts Of Ourselves We Leave With Former Lovers . . . 1

Penknife 2

The Derry Street Trials 3

How I Learned To Speak Cat 5

I Confess My Sins To The Electronic Scales 6

How To Bake A Gingerbread Girl 7

The End Of The End Of The Pier Show 8

An Intrusion Of Cockroaches 9

TripAdvisor™ Reviews For The Overlook Hotel 10

The Conjurer's Apprentice 13

Morning Has Broken 14

Afterwards 15

Snow Domes And Care Homes 16

Anniversary 17

Plait 18

London Plane 19

The Circus Of Possibilities 20

Dragonish 22

The Ghosts Of Hitch-Hikers 23

How To Fly Kites On Wordless Days 24

Emergency Room 25

Acknowledgements 27

About the poet 28

About the Emma Press 28

The Parts Of Ourselves We Leave With Former Lovers

Hush, hush my little sunflower, such noise
at such an hour, I thought – well, never mind
now what I thought – be soothed. The other ladies
of the house are sleeping, you do not want them
trampling down here in their bare faces before noon.
But what's this package at your feet, the one that seeps
like oil? An ear! There, there, it is a shock I know,
but not the worst we've seen. You give them locks
of hair, the illusion of desire, but some, perhaps those
who cannot pay in full – or see the world in strange shadows –
have this urge to give much more. Severine received a finger
once. The fat signet ring attached like a tourniquet.
The smeared gold, we said, reminded us of summer sunsets
over Arles. And Babette, she swears she could string
charm bracelets from hearts proffered on plates. Then Marie,
remember the English gentleman, the one with the cane,
the shriek she gave when she found his –
But look, you are upset again. Let's wrap it back up
in the cloth – carefully – not to disturb the perfect whorl,
or pattern of the blood stippled on the lobe.
Look at the raggedness of this edge. It's not just eyes
that let us peep into the thoughts of men. Take it upstairs
to the cabinet – the *Wunderkammer* –
that is beside my bed. We keep such trinkets
in the drawers. It was moved from Claudine's room –
the sound of souls tapping against the wood,
like palsied bluebottles she said, kept her awake
and disturbed the night-time callers.

Penknife

It was a double-page colour spread:
the man, the rock, the penknife
used in the desert to sever his own arm.

I worried at phrases:
'torn edge', 'widening wound'
like a tongue prodding an ulcer.

He had to break the bone before he could
slice through. I rolled this fact
around my mouth for hours.

At that point I didn't know which way
I would be split: hip to hip or vaginal tearing,
both unimaginable

unlike the man and his bluntish penknife,
the Utah sun, a body heat of rock,
sick smell of seeping cactus,

the yellow marrow cradling the bone,
the sand rust red, the scree, the sweat, the dust
and hour after hour after hour, sawing.

The Derry Street Trials

If she crooks a knowing smile your way
to draw out thoughts that itch within,
then she's a witch.

Scrutinise her dress. If it's raggedy,
hem unstitched or wanton split too high,
then she's a witch.

If you can see the bones of her,
a jut of question marks, a lack of marrow,
then she's a skinny witch.

They are the worst. Though many shape-shift,
disguise their witchy forms
in outsize black and formless grey,

roll malicious intent, year after year,
in thick fat, like the truffling pigs
they want to turn you into.

If you see such figures in the tented dark,
laughing at the night while gathering its riches,
beware. They're all likely witches.

Mark her hair; if there are silver streaks
– known as devil's moonshine – it's a sure sign
she's an accomplished witch.

If she has no children. Or too many.
Leaves them a-bed while she slips out
to conjure coins from the beamy air,

or stays at home, bricked behind her walls
without a man to breathe life in her fire,
then she's a witch

or as good as, by any rational reckoning.
Watch her by the water:
how she skirts the millpond.

How I Learned To Speak Cat

We pleased ourselves.

> Came and went at odd hours
> but were always watchful.

There was you
sleek as the night
pooling yourself into a chair

> or stretched out on a bed
> staking the morning.

And me tongue-tied
in the grammar of cool.

> You taught me to resist
> the pull of a collar

that whiskered awareness
of where you were

> – or weren't – in a room
> in a voice of black fur.

I slunk around you
with the weight of a shadow.

> Our time a dark square
> where we toyed
> with the small things of happiness

then grew bored.

> In the end there was nothing
> domestic about you at all.

In the shift of your bones
the smile that you left

> was all jaguar.

I Confess My Sins To The Electronic Scales

It speaks a language of loss I understand:
  the scantness of half teaspoons of salt,
      a promise of absolution in a row of zeros.

It knows that stones and pounds exist
  outside the realm of number. Tell me, it says,
      how they feel weighed down in your pocket.

I try to remember, conjure a time of glut:
  the carelessness of forkfuls, a slick of fat
      across the lips, ooze of caramel.

And in this act I am unburdened,
  the pebbles inside my mouth loosen,
      drum like cherry stones in a spittoon.

It's like building cairns, some marker
  to show how far we've come on the stainless surface.
      A speak-your-weight monotone

reaches across the darkness, offers forgiveness.
  We surrender ourselves each morning
      to its red-eyed judgement. Soon we'll weigh

no more than paper souls. Everything is connected now:
  the knives in the kitchen drawer
      itch to cut and slice; an unlit fridge

humming its psalms of less and less rocks me to sleep,
  to dream hollow bones of birds, the pelvis of an angel
      so light the air shines through.

How To Bake A Gingerbread Girl

Theobald's, Kettering: 1986-1989

Paint blue icing on her fingertips,
fingers that could snap with cold,

dipped into fridges and glass chillers,
placing cockleshell cakes in pretty rows.

Tie back her hair, dress her in sexless tabards,
dab with jam. Press glacé cherries on her cheeks

when delivery men proffer French stick bouquets
with winked asides about what's just risen

and is fresh enough to eat. Make her strong:
by fifteen she'll haul a tray of farmhouse loaves,

guide bread through slicers without alarm.
Let Saturdays fly from the shelves

in a blitz of crumbs, the dirty grit of sugar.
Knead into her the 26 times table,

that baker's trick of twisting a paper bag closed
so it holds intact delicate layers of hope.

Leave her to prove herself on moonlit mornings,
December nosed to the window,

side-by-side with other gingerbread girls,
tea cupped in frosted hands, backs to the warming oven.

The End Of The End Of The Pier Show

Call it the Titanic Spirit: tonight
we have a show to end all shows,
kicked off by our teenage xylophonist
performing 'Flight of the Bumblebee' blindfold.
Be dazzled as El Niño, East Anglia's premier
flamenco troop, perform their showstopper routine –
testament to our unshaken belief
in Victorian riveting, balustrades and glitter balls.
Yes, we have stood by, watched struts
that held up Yarmouth's ice-cream shops erode,
waved goodbye to penny-slot telescopes
sloshed away in last year's high spring tide.
But your tears are now no longer enough
to resalinate the oceans – so tonight
let's raise the roof of the Cromer Pavillon:
Resist the Great Storm Surge!
It may be too late for the Andaman Islands,
but money raised from ticket sales
will help those forced to flee bungalows
on the English Riviera.
And if we become unmoored midway,
drift out on this boardwalk ark to darker seas,
don't panic, ladies & gentlemen,
our Michael Barrymore tribute act is first aid trained.
Enjoy our award-winning stage hypnotist.
The house band – the King Canuters –
will play loud and long into the night,
as we sail on, towards uncertain morning.

An Intrusion Of Cockroaches

we are unskittled
tip-
    tap-
      top inheritors
of the skank sun
see how it sheens   off us glossblacks
  as we come
          and come
            and come
all topple legs
praising the give   of cracks
in the overspill
              of us
slickly   as oil seep   spreading

o little us   wild with sugar rot
it whips us up   high notes
wavering the   sicksy air
  race you
     race you
        race you for it
zigzag walls
      and carpet roiling floors
with our cravering
click
   click eye-swizzle screens
all   blurrydrunk
with scurfy
            flakes
of mush moon   snow

TripAdvisor™ Reviews For The Overlook Hotel

"We didn't want to leave!"

◉◉◉◉◉

Charming staff, traditional service,
Lloyd serves a generous bourbon on the rocks
and the cutlery is always spit spot polished.
It's the kind of place you settle into, end up loving.
In fact, our girls kicked up such a god-forsaken fuss
when it was time to leave, we decided to extend our visit.
TheGradyBunch

"Plumbing Problems"

◉◯◯◯◯

The hotel management needs to undertake
extensive improvements. My room –137 –
had visible water damage from plumbing issues
in the suite above. The lifts were filthy.
The maze closed without explanation
and the mini-bar was a joke. What desperate
color-blind sales rep drinks *red* rum?
Next year I'll be booking somewhere else
for Colorado's orthodontist convention.

"Terrible Vacation!"

◉ ○ ○ ○ ○

This was my worst vacation ever. Rooms were cramped
and the geometric wallpaper that lined
the maze-like corridors had what I can only describe
as a claustrophobic leaning.
Our bathroom window jammed,
while the doors were cardboard thin,
failing to keep out the din from the 1920s ballroom
– or my husband.
WendyRabbit

The Management of The Overlook Hotel responded to this review:
Dear Guest, Thank you for choosing our hotel
and taking time to share your comments.
We're sorry you didn't fully enjoy your stay.
We'd like to reassure you steps are underway
to address the problems you experienced
with the ~~axe-wielding maniac~~ bathroom window.

"Flexible check-in"

◉ ◉ ◉ ○ ○

Reminds me of the
Hotel California –
with blood-smeared snow boots.
DullBoy

"Family getaway"
●●○○○
The 'Little Boulders' creche was ill-equipped
(<u>one</u> trike!) and attended
by the most ghastly/ghostly kids.
Though you couldn't fault the generous opening hours,
you could leave your children
to play forever for no extra charge.
Tony

"Not what I expected, unfortunately"
●○○○○
What happened to the topiary?
TheRealSKing, Maine

"Marvellous Views"
●●●●○
Gloomy exterior, but panoramic views across the Rockies.
Its seclusion makes this Hotel a great retreat
for yoga enthusiasts or would-be novelists –
though the white-outs aren't ideal
for those with alcohol dependency, mental health issues
or a tendency towards cabin fever.
Still, remaining yoga enthusiasts should note
the caretaker cooks up a sublime omelette.

"Dated Decor"
●●●○○
Man, I still have nightmares about those carpets.
StanleyK

The Conjurer's Apprentice

I cook white rabbit stew, serve it on spinning plates,
strum a deck for the Jack of Hearts,
trump it with a fist of aces.

I am the original vanishing woman
in the box with the false floor.
The knife-thrower's assistant who lobs one back,

a world-renowned reverse escapologist.
Watch me slip on this straightjacket in under a minute,
triple lock myself inside a trunk

and while you're picking at the hasp, I am behind you,
plastic carnations in my hand,
quite giddy on these sawn-off legs.

Morning Has Broken

The milk cried on the doorstep. We toasted blackbirds,
crunched their burnt wings. Watched jam drip
through the egg timer.

Was it eight already? Outside overcoats
and umbrellas quick-stepped the wind.
No-one could tell the time from the telephone

having done its worst, it bit its tongue. We washed faces
in cold light that rained from the ceiling,
knew you could drown in an empty bath.

The great tractor wheels of the day lay on their side.
The engine rusted in parts, like a jigsaw we'd had
of The Haywain. It was all corners. No-one knew where to start.

We cut up newspapers for small talk. Snapped lumps
off the morning and evening stars,
dissolved them in the multiplying flower vases

overflowering with black tea. Our hands
clumsy as hooks as we pinned headaches
to our faces for smiles.

Afterwards

You can't look at them straight at first, these bloody angels,
burning. So they're banished to the newly-acquired spare room

to play backgammon. They don't seem to be in any rush.
Hosts of them throng the hall and landing. Places where you don't stop much.

From the understairs a useless music: a choir
with tennis racquet harps, singing a song to heal a severed limb.

You've watched one watch a tap drip, drip for hours
while you scraped the limescale from your face.

There are so many of them. They're huge; no one tells you that.
They fill the shapes of old armchairs, raiments draped

like antimacassars, Gabriel's wings tucked into a coffee table.
To find a sleep of sorts you count halos looping through the wallpaper

until it's just a pattern, one you can't quite follow.
They are never entirely gone. A hand reaching from a recipe book

pauses you to drop three months of quiet. Some hang
in closets, feathering memories between the winter coats.

One day you'll see them thunder someone else's skies:
the woman three doors down, who, when you knock

to ask if she's all right, answers with splintered breath,
a winged look in her eyes.

Snow Domes And Care Homes

There was snow in the night again, a light dusting,
enough to make strangers of the furniture.
In the glittered morning sun she still expects
her dresser and the jewellery box to rise out of the meltwater,

not these strangers, this blank-faced furniture.
Icicles drip from picture rails, a ticking clock. Time to wake up,
rise from the meltwater, dig out the dresser, her jewellery box
memories, buried like early snowdrops

or snow drips, the icy tick of railing clocks: time to get up,
negotiate the black ice sheeting the floor
(so difficult to dig out buried snowdrops),
easy though to lose your footing, slip from one day to the next

skating along the ice sheeting the floor. She needs to negotiate
black spots in conversations, names and faces
slip too easily, lose their footings from one day to the next.
In this weather sound carries far at night, from years ago

a name or face lights up black spots of conversation,
like constellations in the northern sky, or a flare
carried far at night through heavy weather, something from years ago
to hold onto. Winter rarely comes alone, its quiet light

flares like consolations in a northern sky.
She expects there is still the the sun, the morning
to hold onto, its quiet light. Winter doesn't come alone,
there was snow in the night again, like dusted glitter.

Anniversary

This is the year everyone forgot
to tiptoe round you. No warning look
shot at the kids: *don't play her up.*
No squeeze on the shoulder.

Six years. If it was a wedding
you'd be unwrapping iron,
something wrought and heavy.
But there's no present. No card

saying sorry for your loss.
Because it still is. Time between
loops back, dissolves
like surgeons' stitches on such days.

She'd have remembered though.
Sent a text or phoned that night,
found some excuse to chat
just to check that you're alright.

Plait

The trick is to hold three braids in two hands
and ignore the logistics of mornings.
Wind the first over the second, then cross

the third over the first, and so on. Don't get cross
as arguments slip like hoarded minutes out of hand.
Flex zen-calmed fingers: remember even school mornings

don't last forever. Focus on this Tuesday morning:
soft nape and collar crease, the wonky plait. Let its criss cross
weave a tender magic, like a proverb handed

across generations, mourning there is not enough time, but
    just enough hands.

London Plane

'Being a non-native hybrid there is no mythology or folklore associated with the London Plane… despite being the capital's most common tree.'
The Woodland Trust

They grow in dark spaces between street lights,
root through concrete, creating heart-stress egg cracks

that unsettle suburban homes. Camouflage bark,
it peels like banknotes, mulch for bluebells

blooming in the shade amid the dogshit.
When the pollen count's thirteen and a sickle moon

pokes through the clouds of diesel fumes
dryads emerge, hesitant at first, dizzy

as Blitz-bombed housewives or wayward clubbers,
shaking out limbs that ache from holding.

They tiptoe past statues stood at park gates
to dance havoc in streets drained of the day's worries.

Some nights you'll hear their laugh: gurgle
of sap rising, riot of leaves

calling beneath the traffic drone, like dreams
of elsewhere you can't quite shift next morning.

The slow-worm to work. Look up! Look up!
Finger-tipped avenues are closing above.

The Circus Of Possibilities

To: Simpkins, Michael
From: Temp Account
Subject: The Circus of Possibilities

Apologies Mr Simpkins, I do not have the details
of this afternoon's meeting. But need to inform you
that a circus train bound for the Caucasus
leaves at 3:48. Will you run away with me?

I've watched you plot mortality assumptions
with care for weeks. But I am now convinced, Mr Simpkins,
these are not calculations for an Excel graph;
they demand to be tested on the steel of a high wire.

If I somersaulted towards you would you catch me Mr
    Simpkins?
I think you would. You can quantify actuarial risk
and yield curves so I'd stake the safety
of my rhinestoned trajectory to those measured hands.

I have informed HR. They will waive your notice period
in lieu of future pension payments.
I'm sure your wife will understand. We'll send her tickets
for the gala performance in St Petersburg.

I have learned English and what a fax is
so new skills will not be difficult for you, Mr Simpkins.
Besides, this climate-controlled air conditioning
is no good at all for your constitution:

you need the bite of winter on your skin,
the struggle to peg down guy ropes in a storm.
Can you hear the steam piano? How its tune speeds up
like madness towards the end?

Log off your computer now: we'll make Ukraine by dawn,
spooned on a goose-down mattress;
wake to the stink of axle grease and toffee apples,
laughing at the growl of tethered lions.

Dragonish

You don't hear them after a while:
that scrape of club-clawed tails across the night,
a comet burst of green and yellow sparks
sky-writing disaster in their wake.

Only, sometimes you stir for no apparent reason
at some odd hour, as an orange flame sweeps the room
igniting the face beside you, as you first knew him,
asleep within the contours of another.

You cannot touch him now, or steal such dream-spilled
treasure. Just watch the second skin of clothes
you shed, slung on a chair, burn with the rage of it
before all is obscured again by shadow.

Follow sleep back into its cave, lullabied
by police sirens, the hum of helicopters,
a steady beat of wings and taloned fingertips
drumming out old love-songs on the skylights.

A fine sprinkling of ash coats each morning,
grey taste of damp so commonplace
we no longer think to mention it. And if
– now and again – we dare admit how tired we are

let's kid ourselves it's airport holding patterns
or the metallic screech of distant trains.

The Ghosts Of Hitch-Hikers

still haunt the A-roads, spectral outposts
on the slipways to major junctions
with their faded signs, smiles running in the rain.

They come on certain evenings, when the miles
pound a headache and dark weather swirls
in headlights, spirits summoned through smoked glass.

Just ahead it's her, unwashed hair and muddy rucksack,
thumbing her way back from a festival,
or off to see some ex-boyfriend in Leeds.

You pull up, just past the bend, swing the door open
and a cold blast of air steps in. It's going your way
so you share the lonely motorway hours.

There were hordes of them once. Boys in Afghan coats
and damp parkas that steamed in the radiator's heat,
splitting four cans of Tartan and a deviation via Mansfield.

The girls' bright chatter full of plans for life beyond
now icy condensation misting the windscreen.
The roads north pulse like veins across the map

you've tucked away inside your head, signalling
each verge, each turning. The car crests the hill
and you can see the lights left on in the town below

like birthday cake candles about to be blown out.

How To Fly Kites On Wordless Days

Find a hill, a view to make your lungs ache,
run with time stitched to your heels
unspooling your cloth-yards of hope
until polka dot ribbons stream behind you.
Do all you can to keep these colours airborne.
Be the friend who'll chuck the cross hatch
high into a blue tomorrow,
laugh at the swerve of sky,
and roll out picnic rugs from rain clouds.
Ignore those holding a finger up
to taste the air. Grab the ropes of days
and sail the bright pendant of them, far as you dare,
in spite of pylons. Don't count the starlings
gathering there, like isobars on nearing horizons.

Emergency Room

for Alison

I can't remember now if Dr Ross ever married
the dark-haired nurse.

All I know is I was the first to arrive;
you listened, and poured the wine.

Then listened again as Alex, then Jo, then Grace
each tucked into the crisps and outrage.

Some things in every episode are the same –
that rookie medic struggling with a central line –

so it must have been Rose who said
men are such fucking idiots,

and Eleanor who rolled her eyes to show
just how much she'd never liked him.

And by the time the defibrillators shocked
the man who'd had the cardiac arrest

– or possibly the carjacker caught in crossfire –
back to life, I felt a little loved again.

Dr Greene was still going to die,
but from the kitchen I could hear you muttering

bastard bastard over the season finale closing credits.

Acknowledgements

Thanks are due to the editors of *The Rialto, The Interpreter's House, Obsessed With Pipework, Under the Radar,* and the online journals *Clear Poetry, And Other Poems, Three Drops from a Cauldron* and *The Fat Damsel,* where some of these poems first appeared.

'Plait' won the Prole Laureate Competition (2013), 'The Parts Of Ourselves We Leave With Former Lovers' was commended in The Battered Moons Poetry Competition (2015), 'Afterwards' was awarded third prize in the Manchester Cathedral Poetry Competition (2016) and 'The End Of The End Of The Pier Show' was shortlisted in the 2016 Live Canon Competition. 'TripAdvisor™ Reviews For The Overlook Hotel' first appeared in *The Very Best of 52* (Nine Arches Press, 2015).

I would like to thank Emma Wright and Rachel Piercey of the Emma Press, for their thoughtful edits and wonderful designs and for making this pamphlet happen. It's been such a pleasure to work on it with you both.

My heartfelt thanks also go to Arvon and The Jerwood Foundation, for selecting me to take part in their mentoring scheme, where I had the good fortune to mentored by the talented and generous Caroline Bird. Thank you Caroline, for all the encouragement and guidance.

I'd also like to thank Jo Bell and Norman Hadley for creating the 52 project and making it such a creative and supportive space. Many of the poems here began life there.

Also thanks to Kim Moore and Suzannah Evans. Some of these poems sprang from workshops they've run for The Poetry School. I'd also like to thank Ken Evans and the other Cwm Cole poets for their feedback and good company.

Finally – and most importantly – thanks to Steve, Susie and Katie, for all their love and support.

About the poet

Emma Simon is from Northamptonshire and now lives in London, where she works part-time as a copywriter and journalist. She was one of the poets chosen for the 2015 Jerwood/Arvon Mentoring scheme and she has been published widely, including in *The Very Best of 52* (Nine Arches Press, 2015) and *Writing Motherhood* (Seren, 2017). She won the Prole Laureate Poetry Competition in 2013 and won third prize in the Manchester Cathedral Poetry Competition in 2016.

About the Emma Press

The Emma Press is an independent publisher dedicated to producing beautiful, thought-provoking books. It was founded in 2012 by Emma Wright in Winnersh, UK, and is now based in Birmingham. Having been shortlisted in both 2014 and 2015, the Emma Press won the Michael Marks Award for Poetry Pamphlet Publishers in 2016.

The Emma Press is passionate about making poetry welcoming and accessible. In 2015 they received a grant from Arts Council England to travel around the country with *Myths and Monsters*, a tour of poetry readings and workshops for children. They are often on the lookout for new writing and run regular calls for submissions to their themed poetry anthologies and poetry pamphlet series.

Sign up to the monthly Emma Press newsletter to hear about their events, publications and upcoming calls for submissions. Their books are available to buy from the online shop, as well as in bookshops.

https://theemmapress.com
http://emmavalleypress.blogspot.co.uk/